CONTENTS

3

What is a tiger?

A tiger is a big, wild cat.

Tigers live in the forests and jungles of Asia.

Tiger

World map

Asia

Lions, leopards and cheetahs are also big cats.

Lion

Leopard

Cheetah

Tigers are the biggest of all the cat family.

What does a tiger look like?

A tiger has orange fur with black stripes.

Every tiger has a different pattern of stripes.

Some tigers are white with blue eyes.

Tigers have big teeth and long whiskers.

They have sharp claws.

Teeth

Meet a tiger cub

This is a tiger cub with his mother.

The mother tiger has two cubs.

The cubs are brothers.

When they are born the tiger cubs cannot see. They are blind.

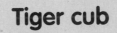

Tiger cub

The mother and the cubs do not live with the father tiger.

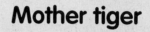

Mother tiger

Tiger eyes

The tiger cub opens his eyes and can see when he is about two weeks old.

At first his eyes are blue.

His eyes change to yellow when he is older.

Looking after the cubs

The mother keeps the cubs safe in a cosy hiding place called a den.

She washes them by licking them with her rough tongue.

She carries them in her mouth.

Tiger cub food

At first the tiger cub and his brother only drink their mother's milk.

Then when they are about six months old they begin to eat meat.

Their mother catches pigs, deer and birds for them to eat.

Hunting

The tiger cubs learn to hunt by watching their mother.

She takes the cubs hunting.

They watch her jump on animals.

They play and jump on each other.

en they jump on small animals.

Growing up

After about two years, the tiger cub leaves his mother.

He lives and hunts on his own.

He marks his part of the forest by scratching trees. This shows other tigers where he lives.

He roars loudly if other tigers come close.

19

Tigers in danger

Tigers are killed for their fur.

The trees in the forests and jungles are cut down to make space for houses and farms.

If the trees are cut down where can the tigers live?

There are only about 8000 tigers left in the world.

21

Thinking and talking about tigers

Where do tigers live?

Who do the tiger cubs live with?

When do the tiger cubs leave their mother?

22

Why are tigers in danger?

What do you think would be the best thing about being a tiger?

What might be the worst thing about being a tiger?

23

Activities

What did you think of this book?

☺ **Brilliant**   ☺ **Good**   😐 **OK**

What was the most interesting fact you found in this book?

● ● ● ● ● ● ● ● ● ● ● ● ●

Which is the odd one out? Why?

cheetah • dog • leopard • lion • tiger

● ● ● ● ● ● ● ● ● ● ● ● ●

Draw a big picture of the head of a tiger and label it. Use these words:

eyes • stripes • teeth • whiskers

● ● ● ● ● ● ● ● ● ● ● ● ●

Who is the author of this book? Have you read *Orang-utan Baby* by the same author?